C000140452

Arweiniad i Lwybr Tref Doc Penfro

Christine Willison &
Dave Ainsworth

Cynhyrchwyd yn 2007 gan
Absolute Design Solutions
www.absolutedesignsolutions.co.uk

© Cyngor Sir Penfro 2007

Cafodd hawliau'r golygyddion eu mynnu yn unol â Deddf
Hawlfreintiau, Dyluniadau a Phatentau 1988.

Cedwir pob hawl. Ni chaniateir atgynhyrchu unrhyw
ran o'r cyhoeddiad hwn na'i gadw na'i osod mewn system
adfer, na'i drosglwyddo mewn unrhyw ddull na thrwy
unrhyw gyfrwng (electronig, mecanyddol, llungopïo,
recordio nac fel arall) heb ganiatâd ysgrifenedig yr awdur.

Argraffwyd a Rhwymwyd yn Ewrop.

Rhagair

Mae'r arweinlyfr hwn yn ddetholiad hefyd o ysgrifennu creadigol gan bobl Doc Penfro am eu tref. Mae'n rhan o brosiect y comisiynwyd tri artist ar ei gyfer i weithio gyda'r gymuned er mwyn creu'r pethau canlynol:

Cyfres o chwech o baneli cerfwedd, wedi ei naddu o Garreg Caerfaddon gan y cerflunydd Perryn Butler ac yna eu bwrw mewn efydd. Mae'r paneli'n mynd â ni trwy hanes y Dociau Brenhinol a'r diwydiant adeiladu llongau.

Yr arlunydd, Robert Jakes , a weithiodd gyda thrigolion Doc Penfro i ymchwilio a chreu, gyda'r plant yn ysgolion Doc Penfro, y dyluniadau ar gyfer pob un o'r placiau troed, a osodir yn y palmant ar hyd y llwybr i nodi mannau diddorol a phwysig ar lwybr y dref ac sydd wedi eu disgrifio yn yr arweinlyfr hwn.

Yr awdur, Dave Ainsworth, a weithiodd gyda phlant ac athrawon ysgolion Doc Penfro, gyda chymdeithasau ysgrifennu yn yr ardal a gyda grwpiau ac unigolion eraill yn y gymuned, i greu toreth o ysgrifennu creadigol sy'n cofnodi rhai o'r digwyddiadau a'r lleoedd mewn barddoniaeth a rhyddiaith.

Roedd hyn yn rhan o brosiect Menter Treftadaeth Treflun Doc Penfro, a noddwyd gan Gronfa Dreftadaeth y Loteri, Cyngor Sir Penfro, Awdurdod Datblygu Cymru a Llywodraeth y Cynulliad, sydd wedi cynorthwyo gydag adfywio Doc Penfro ac adnewyddu llawer o'r adeiladau hanesyddol sydd yma.

Christine Willison
Swyddog Celfyddydau
Cyngor Sir Penfro
Chwefror 2007

Cydnabyddiaeth

Grŵp Llywio	Menter Treftadaeth Treflun Doc Penfro
Perryn Butler	Cerflunydd
Robert Jakes	Arlunydd
Dave Ainsworth,	Awdur
Christine Willison	Swyddog Celfyddydau Cyngor Sir Penfro
Mark Thomas	Swyddog Amgueddfeydd Cyngor Sir Penfro
AB Fine Art	Ffowndri
David Jones	Cyngor Tref Doc Penfro ac Ymddiriedolaeth Amgueddfa Doc Penfro

John Williams
David James
John Davies
Ron Watts
R. Haggar

Plant ac Athrawon;

    Ysgol Albion Square
    Ysgol Gynradd Pennar
    Ysgol y Babanod, Pennar
    Ysgol Gymunedol Doc Penfro
    Ysgol Gatholig y Santes Fair
    Ysgol Gyfun Bush

1. Y 'Carmarthenshire'-
The 'Carmarthenshire'
(Library - Llyfrgell)

Agorwyd y Llyfrgell, a godwyd ar hen dir llanw, ym1987. Hen enw Water Street, yr heol rhwng y llyfrgell a swyddfa'r heddlu, oedd Shore Street, sy'n ein hatgoffa pa mor bell yr arferai'r llanw ymestyn. Yn y fan hon yr adeiladwyd llawer o longau, yn cynnwys y llong fasnach 'Carmarthenshire' a adeiladwyd ym1865. Hon oedd y llong gyntaf o'i math i fynd i mewn i borthladd Yokohama yn Japan. Yn ogystal â'i llwyth o lo o Gaerdydd, ar y llong hefyd oedd y merched gorllewinol cyntaf a welodd pobl Japan erioed. Yn fuan wedi i wraig a merch y capten lanio, gwelwyd lluniau o ffasiynau Ewropeaidd ar amrywiaeth o lestri dwyreiniol.

2. Tŷ'r Pwmp -
The Pump House

Mae'r adeilad rhyfedd hwn o frics coch yn sefyll ar ganol y gylchfan sy'n arwain i Western Way. Er iddo gael ei godi'n wreiddiol i bwmpio carthion o'r dref i'r Dociau, ni wnaeth hyn erioed fel mae'n digwydd. Ni welwyd unrhyw angen o gwbl am system bwmpio o'r fath!

Yn ei amser, mae'r adeilad hardd hwn wedi bod yn dŷ cwrdd, yn glwb pysgota ac yn eglwys.

Mae hyn hefyd ar bwys safle Gwesty Pier House a fomiwyd yn ystod yr Ail Ryfel Byd.

3. Sioe Orllewin Gwyllt Byfflo Bill - Buffalo Bill's Wild West Show

Anodd yw dychmygu bod un o ddifyrwyr mwyaf rhan olaf y bedwaredd ganrif ar bymtheg wedi ymweld â'r dref ddociau hon, ond mae'n hollol wir fod Byfflo Bill wedi gwneud hynny!

Daethpwyd â Sioe Orllewin Gwyllt Byfflo Bill yn ei holl ogoniant i'r lle hwn Mai'r 14eg 1903. Dechreuwyd y sioe, portread anferthol o'r Gorllewin Gwyllt, a oedd yn cynnwys 500 o farchogion, gyda gorymdaith o Orsaf Penfro i'r safle hwn yn Bierspool. Yr arweinydd oedd dyn mawr y sioe ei hun, William F. Cody, neu wrth ei enw arall, Buffalo Bill. Un o'r prif atyniadau oedd amrywiaeth o gampau marchogaeth gydag Americanwyr Brodorol, ymarferion saethu chwim ac amrywiaeth o arddangosiadau gyda gauchos o Dde America, dynion o lwyth y Bedwyn a Chosaciaid o Rwsia.

4. Mynwent Filwrol Llanion - Llanion Military Cemetery

Ychydig o bobl yn unig sy'n sylweddoli mai hon yw'r unig Fynwent Filwrol yng Nghymru. Dyma orffwysfa olaf dynion y lluoedd arfog a'u perthnasau a fu farw tra'r oeddent yn gwasanaethu yn y dref garsiwn. Mae hon, o'r golwg yn ystâd dai Llanion, yn un o drysorau cudd Doc Penfro!

Chwiliwch am res o ddau fedd ar bymtheg yn rhan ddeheuol y fynwent. Y rhain yw beddi'r milwyr a fu farw mewn ffrwydrad damweiniol wrth ymarfer gyda dulliau o ddiarfogi meiniau. Digwyddodd hyn yr 28ain Ebrill 1942. Y dynion a laddwyd oedd naw Peiriannydd Brenhinol, pedwar o Ffinwyr Albanaidd y Brenin ei Hun a phedwar a oedd yn gwasanaethu gyda'r Chorfflu'r Arloeswyr.

A dyma beth anhygoel ynglŷn â'r stori – y diwrnod hwnnw llwyddodd un swyddog i ddianc rhag marwolaeth anochel pan aeth o'r lle trychinebus hwnnw i ateb y ffôn!

5. Y Gwersyll Cytiau -
The Hut Camp

Yma un tro roedd y Gwersyll Cytiau, a elwid yn Farics Llanion yn ddiweddarach. Yn wreiddiol, codwyd y barics hyn, a allai ddal cymaint â 1000 o ddynion, mewn chwe wythnos! Mae catrodau troedfilwyr o bob rhan o'r wlad wedi byw yn y barics hyn. Codwyd y barics brics coch a welwn yma heddiw yn ddiweddarach ym 1906. Yn ystod yr Ail Ryfel Byd hwn oedd cartref milwyr Americanaidd 110fed Catrawd Troedfilwyr yr Unol Daleithiau, ac oherwydd hynny cafwyd ymweliad gan Bencadfridog y Cynghreiriaid, Dwight D. Eisenhower a gyrhaeddodd yma yn Llanion ym 1944.

Mae'r Barics wedi ei addasu erbyn hyn yn breswylfa, ac yn yr adeilad lle bu swyddogion yn byw, nawr mae Awdurdod Parc Cenedlaethol Arfordir Penfro a Chyngor Cefn Gwlad Cymru.

6. Hobbs Point –
Hobbs Point

Adeiladwyd Hobbs Point gan brentisiaid ym 1829 i fod yn adran 'Offeru' ar gyfer llongau a adeiladwyd yn y Dociau. Defnyddiwyd cloch blymio i osod y sylfeini.

Pan ddaeth rhwydwaith ffyrdd Telford yma o'r diwedd ym 1837, daeth Doc Penfro yn dref bost ac felly yn lle pwysig ar gyfer cludo'r post rhwng Iwerddon a Phrydain Fawr.

Cyd codi Pont Cleddau, yn gyntaf roedd fferi i deithwyr ac yna fferi ceir yn croesi rhwng Hobbs Point a Neyland.

7. Cae Ffair –
Fairground

Bu rasys ceffylau ac ambell i ffair ar 'Watery Meadows' ac mae'r traddodiad yn dal yn fyw heddiw.

8. Stryd Flaen–
Front Street

Pan fyddwch yn cerdded ar hyd Front Street, craffwch yn ofalus ar rifau 25 i 28 oherwydd y rhain, yn ôl pob tebyg, yw'r tai cyntaf a godwyd yn Noc Penfro. Mae llawer wedi newid ac anodd yw credu y bu saith o dafarnau un tro ar yr heol gymharol gwta hon i dorri syched cannoedd o weithwyr y dociau! Ar ben hyn oll, arferai merched o Langwm lywio eu cychod yma i werthu pysgod o wahanol fathau.

9. Amgueddfa Twr y Gwn – Guntower Museum

Mae'r adeilad trawiadol hwn o gerrig, a godwyd ym 1849 – 50 am £9,230, ym mhen gorllewinol Front Street. Mae'r Twr Gwn 'Caergaint' yma yn un o saith yn unig trwy'r byd i gyd, ac mae'r saith yma ar lan yr Aber. Ei ddiben gwreiddiol oedd gwrthsefyll llongau'r gelyn ond erbyn hyn amgueddfa'r dref ydyw ac mae'n werth ei weld heb os nac oni bai.

Paneli Efydd

Heibio i'r gornel ar fur y Dociau, gallwch weld chwech o baneli cerfwedd. Naddwyd hwy o Garreg Caerfaddon gan y cerflunydd.

Perryn Butler ac yna eu bwrw mewn efydd. Maent yn disgrifio hanes adeiladu cychod yn Noc Penfro.

Magwyd y cerflunydd yn Noc Penfro. Ei thad oedd Harbwr Feistr y Frenhines yn Noc Penfro rhwng 1953 a 1957.

Panel 1
Paterchurch Point   (Y Cyfnod Sioraidd)

Panel 2
Daw fy llong un diwrnod   (Rhan gyntaf Oes Fictoria)

Panel 3
Lansio'r 'Osborne'   (Canol Oes Fictoria)

Panel 4
Pwno rhybedi yn y sied fawr (Rhan olaf Oes Fictoria)

Panel 5
Diwrnod Cyflog 1907   (Y Cyfnod Edwardaidd)

Panel 6
Trawiad Unionsyth 1941   (Siôr IV)

10. Arwydd Lloches Rhag Bomiau – Air Raid Shelter Sign

Mae'r adeilad hynod ar ben Commercial Row yn enghraifft wych o flaen siop o flynyddoedd cynnar yr 20fed ganrif. Bu'n gefndir i nifer o olygfeydd yn y rhaglen deledu boblogaidd, The Onedin Line.

Y drws nesaf i siop y fferyllydd, safai banc cyntaf Doc Penfro, Banc Aberdaugleddau (The Milford Haven Bank). Gyferbyn â'r siop, bydd llygaid craff yn sylwi bod arwydd lloches rhag bomiau o adeg y rhyfel yn sownd mewn coeden.

11. Capel Y Garsiwn –
Garrison Chapel

Credir mai Capel y Garsiwn neu Capel y Dociau, a godwyd ym 1831, yw'r unig eglwys Glasurol Sioraidd yng Nghymru.

Adeiladwyd yn arbennig ar gyfer y milwyr oedd yn byw yma ac un o'i addolwyr mwyaf adnabyddus oedd y Cadfridog Gordon o Gartŵm a oedd yn gwasanaethu gyda'r Peirianwyr Brenhinol. Nodweddion mwyaf diddorol y capel yw ei do crwm a'r clochdy. Cafodd y gloch a grogai yma ar y cychwyn ei bwrw yn Sbaen, a chipiwyd hi oddi ar long ryfel Sbaenaidd!

Daeth y capel yn ddiweddarach yn Theatr y Garsiwn, cyn iddo fynd â'i ben iddo. Roedd pawb wrth ei fodd pan ddaeth y gwaith o adfer yr adeiladwaith i ben, gyda nawdd Cronfa Dreftadaeth y Loteri, yn 2005.

12. Awyrennau Môr 'Sunderland' – Sunderland Flying Boats

Ym 1930, cafodd y rhan fwyaf o'r dociau ei throsglwyddo o'r Morlys i'r Weinyddiaeth Awyr. Y flwyddyn wedyn, sefydlodd y llu awyr ganolfan awyrennau môr lle bu awyrennau môr Southampton sgwadron 210. Ym 1938, cyrhaeddodd awyrennau môr Sunderland cyntaf y sgwadron - yr awyren y cysylltir Doc Penfro â hi fwyaf. Yn ystod yr Ail Ryfel Byd gwnaeth y Sunderlands y gwaith pwysig o amddiffyn Gosgorddion Prydain rhag Llynges yr Almaen.

13. Terfynfa'r Fferi – Ferry Terminal

Pedair awr yn unig yw'r daith i Iwerddon o derfynfa'r fferi yma yn Noc Penfro. Y llong sy'n mynd â chi yno yw'r Isle of Innishmore, y llong fferi fwyaf ond un yn Ewrop.

14. Iard Longau'r Llynges Frenhinol – Royal Naval Dockyard

Yn eu hanterth yn ystod nawdegau'r bedwaredd ganrif ar bymtheg, roedd y Dociau Brenhinol gyda'r mwyaf yn y byd, yn cyflogi mwy na 3,000 o bobl. Mae mwy na 250 o longau'r Llynges Frenhinol a phump o longau hwylio brenhinol wedi eu hadeiladu yma dros y blynyddoedd. Mae Doc Penfro'n gallu ymffrostio mai yma y gwnaethpwyd llawer o bethau am y tro cyntaf, fel y llong ryfel ager gyntaf, HMS Tartar a'r llong ryfel gyntaf i'w gyrru gyda sgriw, HMS Conflict.

15. Tŵr Paterchurch – Paterchurch Tower

Yn hŷn ôl pob tebyg na'r drydedd ganrif ar ddeg, dyma'r adeilad hynaf yn Noc Penfro. Mae'n enghraifft wych o dŵr gyda neuadd ar y llawr cyntaf ond mae ei ddiben gwreiddiol yn dipyn o ddirgelwch. Gwyddom ei fod unwaith yn eiddo i Farchogion Sant Ioan o Gaersalem. A oedd yn eglwys, yn dŵr gwylio neu'n fferm? Efallai ei fod yn gyfuniad o'r tri. Cafwyd rhagor o dystiolaeth, mae'n siŵr, y gallai fod yn eglwys, pan estynnwyd muriau'r dociau ym 1844. Wrth wneud hyn, gwelwyd bod hen fynwent ar bwys y tŵr.

Pater oedd enw Doc Penfro cyn sefydlu'r dociau.

16. Rasys Beiciau Peni-ffardding –
Penny Farthing Bike Races

Yn y ffair a fu ar y safle hwn ym 1902, cynhaliwyd
Rasys Beiciau Peni-ffardding.

17. Llongau Tanfor Y Rhyfel Byd Cyntaf - WWI Submarines

Yn ogystal â'r nifer fawr o longau a adeiladwyd yma yn y dociau, mae siediau torpidos Whitehouse yn ein hatgoffa o'r nifer fawr o longau tanfor a adeiladwyd yma yn ystod y Rhyfel Byd Cyntaf. Yn eu plith oedd yr L10 anffodus a adeiladwyd yn Noc Penfro ym 1918. Yn ystod profion môr ger St Ann's Head, trawodd y llong danfor ar y gwaelod a methodd â chodi. Yn fuan iawn y clywyd am ei thrafferthion yn y dociau a bu gwylwyr pryderus yn disgwyl iddi ddychwelyd yn y gwynt a'r glaw. O'r diwedd, wedi oriau maith ac er rhyddhad i bawb, llwyddodd i ddod lan.

Ond gwae a ddaeth i'w rhan eto'n fuan, fodd bynnag, ac ychydig fisoedd wedi hynny, suddwyd hi gan long ryfel o'r Almaen!

18. Balwnau Amddiffyn – Barrage Balloons

Dyma safle un o'r Balwnau Amddiffyn niferus a oedd wedi eu clymu ar hyd a lled y dref yn ystod yr Ail Ryfel Byd. Bu cryn dipyn o drafferth gydag un o'r rhain ym Mhennar pan ddaeth yn rhydd o'i angor ger Eglwys Padrig Sant a dechreuodd hedfan uwchben Bufferland. Chwalodd ambell i gorn simnai cyn y gellid ei dynnu'n ôl.

19. Y Capten Watkin Owen Pell – Captain Watkin Owen Pell

Un o oruchwylwyr mwyaf lliwgar y Dociau yn ystod y bedwaredd ganrif ar bymtheg oedd y Capten Watkin Owen Pell. Collodd ei goes wrth ymladd yn erbyn y Ffrancwyr ym 1800 a chafodd goes bren yn ei lle. Roedd yn ddisgyblwr llym a byddai'n arfer cadw golwg ar waith ei ddynion trwy wylio gyda'i delesgop o ben Bryn y Barics. Roedd ei ful, a oedd yn ei gludo o amgylch y Dociau, wedi ei hyfforddi mor dda, y byddai'n mynd ag ef lan y pomprennau ac ar fyrddau'r llongau a oedd yn cael eu hadeiladu.

20. Barics Amddiffynadwy –
Defensible Barracks

Mae'r Barics Amddiffynadwy yn adeilad rhestredig rhestr II a godwyd i amddiffyn y dociau rhag ymosodiad o'r tir. Cychwynnwyd yr adeilad ym 1841 a'i gwblhau ym 1846. Honnir bod cynllun cyffredinol y barics wedi ei ddylanwadu gan gaerwaith Eidalaidd o'r unfed ganrif ar bymtheg. Yn wreiddiol, enw'r barics oedd Barics Treowen ac o'r fan yma, dwywaith y dydd, byddai canon yn tanio'n wag er mwyn rhoi gwybod i bawb oedd heb oriawr yn y dref ei bod hi un ai'n hanner dydd neu'n hanner awr wedi naw gyda'r nos. Daeth yr ergyd am 9.30 yn rhybudd i'r merched lleol a oedd 'mas yn caru' ei bod yn amser mynd adref. Clywyd y gwn dydd a'r gwn nos am y tro olaf yn ystod y 20'au.

Tra'r oedd yn gwasanaethu gydag Iwmyn Dug Caerhirfryn, bu'r actor cymeriadau poblogaidd Arthur Lowe (a oedd yn actio'r Capten Mainwaring yn y gyfres Dad's Army) yma yn y Barics Amddiffynadwy.

21. Tân Tanc Olew –
Oil Tank Fire

Adeiladodd y Morlys nifer o danciau olew enfawr ar y safle hwn yn Llanreath ym 1927. Yn ystod y rhyfel, ymosododd tair awyren o'r Almaen ar y tanciau hyn, dydd Llun Awst y 19eg 1940. Roedd y tân yn sgil hynny yn un o goelcerthi mwyaf y rhyfel. Bu'n wenfflam wyllt am dair wythnos a bu 650 o ddynion tân o frigadau ym mhob rhan o'r wlad yn brwydro yn ei erbyn. Cafodd 11 o'r 17 o danciau eu difa'n llwyr a bu farw pump o ddynion tân o Gaerdydd. Mae cofeb iddynt i'w gweld yng nghanol y Maes Golff.

22. Ffrwydrynnau Tanfor – Submarine Mines

Adeiladodd y Llywodraeth storfa dorpidos ac arfdy ger y lan ar bwys Aber Pennar ym 1875. Cynhaliwyd profion yno ar dorpidos a ffrwydrynnau tanfor, yr unig rai o'r fath yng Nghymru. Ar y safle hwn hefyd yr oeddent yn cadw'r holl offer ar gyfer taenu ffrwydrynnau ar yr Aber i gyd.

Wedi'r Ail Ryfel Byd, nid oedd angen safle'r storfa dorpidos. Gwerthwyd y tir a'i droi'n Wersyll Gwyliau Parc Pennar. Mae hwnnw wedi cau erbyn hyn.

23. Cwch Fferi –
Ferry Boat

Ar y fferi o Bentlass i Bennar y byddai gwragedd y ffermwyr yn amlach na pheidio yn arfer dod â'u cynnyrch i'r farchnad yn Noc Penfro. Roedd gweithwyr a oedd yn byw ar ochr arall yr afon yn arfer croesi arno hefyd.

Digwyddodd trychineb ar Chwefror yr 8fed 1889 pan suddodd y fferi gan foddi pob un o'r naw oedd arno. Roedd dyn y fferi, John Jones a'i was ifanc yn dod yn ôl gyda saith o wragedd ar y cwch a oedd wedi bod yn y farchnad. Roedd y dŵr wedi bod yn arw ac roedd y llanw yn gwthio yn erbyn gwynt mawr. Dyfarniad y cwest oedd "bod yr ymadawedig a'r rhai oedd gydag ef wedi marw wedi i'r cwch droi drosodd yn ddamweiniol."

24. Jacobs Pill -
Jacobs Pill

L lygriad yw Pill o'r gair Cymraeg 'pwll'.

Byddent wedi gweld llongau morladron yn mynd heibio i'r fan yma ar eu ffordd lan i Gei Penfro.

Sefydlwyd Iard Gychod Jacob's Pill gan Syr Edward Reed yn 1874 i gystadlu yn erbyn y Dociau Brenhinol. Wedi ei ethol yn AS i Fwrdeistref Penfro, cyflawnodd ei addewid o greu iard longau, gan gynnig llawer o swyddi i weithwyr a gollodd eu gwaith yn ddiweddar. Roedd Syr Edward Reed, a gymerodd ran yn y gwaith o gynllunio'r Llong Hwyliau Frenhinol 'Osborne', yn gynllunydd cychod prysur iawn. Efallai mai'r llong enwocaf a adeiladwyd yma erioed oedd yr Hiei, gosgorddlong a adeiladwyd i Lynges Japan ac a lansiwyd ym 1877. Erbyn diwedd y bedwaredd ganrif ar bymtheg, roedd yr iard wedi cau a rhwng y ddau Ryfel Byd agorwyd Ysbyty Neilltuo yma.

25. Capel Bethania –
Bethany Chapel

Pan ddechreuodd y Dociau a thwf cyflym tref newydd Doc Penfro, codwyd eglwysi a chapeli i fodloni galwadau cynyddol addolwyr y dref. Y rhai cyntaf i wneud hyn oedd y Bedyddwyr a gododd Capel Bethania ym 1818. Hwy oedd y sefydliad Cristnogol cyntaf yn Noc Penfro i godi addoldy. Codwyd yr adeilad cyntaf gan weithwyr gwirfoddol ac roedd lle i eistedd ynddo ar gyfer 350.

Ym 1877, gwelwyd bod angen adeilad newydd ar gyfer gofynion y gynulleidfa gynyddol. Ychwanegwyd ysgoldy ym 1904-5.

26. Neuadd y Farchnad –
The Market Hall

Adeiladwyd Neuadd y Farchnad ym 1826 a'i phrynu gan Gyngor y Fwrdeistref ym 1881. Un adeg, cynhelid sioeau amrywiaeth yn yr hen lys barn.

Diddorol yw gweld yr hyn beiriant stampiau post ar y wal ddwyreiniol.

Adnewyddwyd y safle cyfan yn ddiweddar gyda chymorth grant treftadaeth y Loteri.

27. Ysgol Sgwâr Albion – Albion Square School

Sgwâr yr Albion oedd canolbwynt Doc Penfro. Agorwyd y Co-op cyntaf yma ym 1893 ac, yn Charlton Terrace gerllaw, oedd Pencadlys Heddlu'r Sir, y carchar a'r pownd.

Ar ganol y sgwâr mae lamp goffa, a godwyd ym 1914 i nodi canmlwyddiant y Dociau Brenhinol.

Ar ochr ddeheuol y sgwâr mae Ysgol Fabanod Sgwâr yr Albion, (wedi cau erbyn hyn), enghraifft ragorol o Ysgol Ford Fictorianaidd. Ysgol ar gyfer merched a babanod oedd hi'n wreiddiol. Arferai'r bechgyn fynd i'r Hen Ysgol Brydeinig yn Heol Meyrick gerllaw.

28. Bysiau Deulawr -
Double Deckers

Roedd gan gwmni Silcox fflyd o fysiau deulawr coch, rhai gyda chadeiriau gwiail. Roedd Ernie James yn yrrwr ac yn berchen ar fws unllawr glas, y 'Pioneer'. Ni fyddai Ernie byth yn ein gadael ni'n sefyll wrth arosfan hyd yn oed os oedd y bws yn llawn hyd y fyl. Roedden ni i gyd yn meddwl y byd o'r hen Ernie – roedd ganddo ddoli taflu llais a byddai'n cymryd rhan mewn cyngherddau lleol. (Gweler *A Scrap of Local History* - Tud 69)

29. Eglwys Gatholig Y Santes Fair – St Mary's RC Church

Yn ôl pob sôn, roedd gweithwyr Catholig y dociau, yr oedd llawer ohonynt yn fewnfudwyr Gwyddelig yn dianc rhag newyn, yn arfer cyfrannu cyflog un diwrnod pob mis er mwyn codi Eglwys y Santes Fair ym 1847. Gweithiodd rhai ohonynt yn ddi-dâl i'w hadeiladu. Diddorol yw gweld y ffenestri lliw sy'n harddu'r wal ddwyreiniol, a osodwyd yno ym 1926. Ar bwys yr eglwys mae bedd y Tad Oliver Murphy a wasanaethodd yn offeiriad yn Eglwys y Santes Fair am 44 o flynyddoedd ac a gladdwyd yno gyda chaniatâd arbennig.

30. Eglwys Rydd Seion –
Zion Free Church

Roedd yr adeilad hardd hwn un tro yn Gapel Wesleaidd. Codwyd ef gyda'r iawndal a gafwyd pan oedd rhaid dymchwel hen gapel y Methodistiaid oherwydd ei fod o fewn pellter penodol o'r safle lle'r oeddent yn mynd i godi'r Barics Amddiffynadwy.

Oherwydd cynnydd y gynulleidfa roedd rhaid ei ehangu ym 1867 i'r adeilad trawiadol sydd yno nawr gyda lle i eistedd ar gyfer 1340 o bobl.

Caewyd y Capel Wesle, fel y gelwid ef erbyn hynny, a'i roi ar werth ym 1986. Cafodd ei brynu a'i 'ailfedyddio' yn Eglwys Rydd Seion.

Cyn hyn, roedd llyfrgell y dref ar lawr isaf y capel hyd nes dyfarnwyd bod yr adeilad yn anniogel i'w ddefnyddio gan y cyhoedd.

31. Sinema'r Grand –
Grand Cinema

Roedd sinema'r Grand ar waelod Heol Meyrick
Isaf. Mae rhan o Ganolfan St Govan's ar y safle
nawr.

32. Neuadd Pater –
Pater Hall

Codwyd Neuadd Pater ar safle Neuadd Ddirwest y dref, a chwalwyd hi gan fomiau yn ystod yr Ail Ryfel Byd. Yn ôl y sôn, pan ffrwydrodd y bomiau, chwythwyd prif ddrysau'r adeilad mas a chafwyd yr allwedd yn ddiweddarach yn Front Street!

Y neuadd yw prif ganolfan adloniant a chymdeithasol y dref ac mae lle i 255 o bobl eistedd ynddi. Yn yr adeilad mae siambr y cyngor, swyddfa Clerc y Dref ac ystafell gwrdd.

33. Capel Bethel –
Bethel Chapel

Pan oedd ar griw anghydffurfiol o gynulleidfa Capel Bethania eisiau eglwys ar wahân, codwyd Capel Bethel yma ganddynt ym 1844. Roedd rhaid ailgodi'r adeilad Neo-gothig hwn, gyda'i 400 o seti, ym 1872 pan chwythodd corwynt nerthol ran o'i do bant.

Ym 1857, Capel Bethel yn ôl pob sôn oedd yr eglwys anghydffurfiol gyntaf yn Sir Benfro gydag 'offeryn bysellog' – sef harmoniwm.

*34. Canolfan y Coroni –
Coronation Centre

Yn ôl yr hanes, sefydlwyd Hen Ysgol Brydeinig Heol Meyrick ym 1901 yn sgil yr anghydffurfiaeth o dan ddylanwad yr Eglwys yn Ysgol Genedlaethol Heol Fictoria. Cafodd yr ysgol ei dymchwel ac ym 1904 codwyd yn ei lle yr adeilad a welwn yno heddiw, sef Ysgol Bechgyn y Coroni. Erbyn heddiw, Canolfan Addysg Bellach y dref yw hi.

Yn yr adeilad mae dau furlun mawr trawiadol sy'n darlunio treftadaeth gyfoethog Doc Penfro. Cafodd y rhain eu creu gan Mr George Lewis a'u paentio gyda chymorth ei fyfyrwyr.

35. Eglwys Blwyf Sant Ioan – St John's Parish Church

Codwyd Eglwys Blwyf Sant Ioan ym 1847. Dylanwadodd yr eglwysi o'r drydedd ganrif ar ddeg yn Ninbych-y-pysgod a Chastellmartin ar ei chynllun cyffredinol. Mae gan yr eglwys hon bymtheg o ffenestri lliw a ddyluniwyd gan C. E. Kemp ac yng Nghapel y Forwyn mae enghreifftiau godidog o wrthgefn allor cerfiedig sy'n gofeb i ddynion Troedfilwyr Ysgafn y Brenin a oedd ym marics Doc Penfro yn ystod y Rhyfel Byd Cyntaf. Ar ben hynny, y tu ôl i'r eglwys, mae bord goffa gyda rhestr o enwau holl ddynion y lluoedd arfog a fu farw yn yr Ail Ryfel Byd.

Cafodd y clychau yn y tŵr trawiadol eu cwblhau ym 1902 er mwyn coffau coroni Edward y Seithfed.

36. Eglwys Sant Andreas – St Andrew's Parish Church

Wedi ei adeiladu ar gynllun Gothig Eidalaidd o galchfeini llwyd sgwâr gyda nodweddion amlwg o frics coch a charreg Caerfaddon, sefydlwyd yr adeilad hwn ym 1866. Mae gan Eglwys Bresbyteraidd Sant Andreas dair ffenestr liw hardd, sy'n beth anarferol mewn eglwys Anghydffurfiol ac roedd lle i eistedd ar gyfer 750 o blant yn ei hislawr mawr lle cynhelid yr Ysgol Sul!

Cafodd yr eglwys ei hadnewyddu'n helaeth ym 1881, yn cynnwys gosod to newydd a gwella acwsteg yr adeilad.

37. Y Parc Coffa – Memorial Park

Agorwyd y Parc Coffa ym 1925 ac mae'n coffau "arwyr Doc Penfro a gwympodd ac a roddodd eu bywydau yn Rhyfel Mawr 1914-18."

Codwyd y giatiau a'r cloc er cof am ddau ddyn ifanc a laddwyd yng nghyrchoedd awyr 1941. Roedd un yn 18 oed a'r llall yn ddim ond 14.

Yn ystod yr Ail Ryfel Byd, cafodd rhan fawr o'r parc ei haredig yn rhan o'r ymgyrch Palu i Fuddugoliaeth. Y bwriad oedd tyfu winwns ond ni thyfodd dim. Yn y pen draw, tybiwyd bod y tir yn anaddas i dyfu unrhyw fath o lysieuyn!

38. W. Haggar – Arloeswr y Sinema – W. Haggar – Pioneer of Cinema

Roedd Arthur William Haggar (1851-1925) yn un o wir arloeswyr y sinema. Roedd hefyd yn ddyn sioe a pherchen ffair. Teithiodd ef a'i deulu mawr ar hyd a lled Prydain yn dod ag adloniant i'r bobl. Yma ym Maes yr Orsaf roedd Fiosgop Trydan, ei waith cwyr a'i sioeau trydanol yn difyrru pobl Doc Penfro yn rheolaidd. Yn ddiweddarach, bu ei wŷr, Len Haggar, yn cadw sinemâu ym Mhenfro, Aberdaugleddau, Aberteifi a Doc Penfro.

39. Gorsaf Reilffordd –
Railway Station

Agorwyd gorsaf Doc Penfro ym 1864, ac roedd yn cynnig tocyn i Ddinbych-y-pysgod yn rhad ac am ddim ar y daith gyntaf. Roedd y rheilffordd yn croesi'r dref ac i mewn i'r dociau. Agorwyd ail gangen i Hobbs Point yn ystod saith degau'r bedwaredd ganrif ar bymtheg. Yr orsaf oedd prif leoliad ffilm a wnaeth Haggar ym 1908 o'r enw The Life and Death of Charles Peace. Nid yn unig yr oedd y ffilm yn cynnwys yr olygfa gwrso gyntaf erioed, a hynny sawl blwyddyn cyn y ffilmiau Keystone Cops mwy adnabyddus, hon hefyd oedd y ffilm gyntaf gyda golygfa farw ynddi. Creodd y ffilm hon, yn seiliedig ar hanes gwir, gynnwrf mawr ac elwodd y teulu Haggar yn fawr iawn arni. Mae'r orsaf yn dal ar agor ac mae ei hen swyddfa ac ystafell aros erbyn hyn yn dafarn.

Guide to Pembroke Dock Town Trail

Edited by Christine Willison
& Dave Ainsworth

Produced in 2007 by Absolute Design Solutions
www.absolutedesignsolutions.co.uk

© 2007 Pembrokeshire County Council

The author's rights have been asserted in accordance with the Copyright, Designs and Patents Act 1988.

All rights reserved. No part of this publication may be reproduced, stored in or introduced into a retrieval system, or transmitted, in any form, or by any means (electronic, mechanical, photocopying, recording or otherwise) without the written permission of the author.

Printed and bound in Europe

Foreword

This guide book is also an anthology of Pembroke Dock people's creative writing about their town. It is part of a project in which three artists were commissioned to work with the community to create the following:

A series of six relief panels, carved in Bath Stone by sculptor Perryn Butler and then cast in bronze. The panels take us through the history of the Royal Dockyard and the shipbuilding industry.

Artist, Robert Jakes who worked with residents of Pembroke Dock to research and create, with children in the schools in Pembroke Dock, the designs for each of the footplates, set into the pavement along the trail to pinpoint places of interest and significance on the town trail and described in this guide book.

Writer, Dave Ainsworth writer who worked with children and staff in Pembroke Dock Schools, with writers groups in the area and with other groups and individuals in the community, to produce a wealth of creative writing, which records some of the events and places in poetry and prose.

This was part of The Pembroke Dock Townscape Heritage Initiative project, funded by Heritage Lottery Funding, Pembrokeshire County Council, The Welsh Development Agency and the Welsh Assembly Government, which has assisted in the regeneration of Pembroke Dock and the refurbishment of many of the historic buildings here.

Christine Willison
Arts Officer
Pembrokeshire County Council
February 2007

Acknowledgements

Steering Group	Pembroke Dock Townscape Heritage Initiative.
Perryn Butler	Sculptor
Robert Jakes	Artist
Dave Ainsworth	Writer
Christine Willison	Arts Officer Pembrokeshire County Council
Mark Thomas	Museums Officer Pembrokeshire County Council
AB Fine Art	Foundry
David Jones	Pembroke Dock Town Council & Pembroke Dock Museum Trust.

John Williams
David James
John Davies
Ron Watts
R Haggar

Children and Staff of;

Albion Square School
Pennar Junior School
Pennar Infants School
Pembroke Dock Community School
St Mary's RC School
Bush Comprehensive School

1. Y 'Carmarthenshire'-
The 'Carmarthenshire'
(Library - Llyfrygell)

The Library, which was built on land once tidal, was opened in 1987. Water Street, the road that separates the library and the police station was once called Shore Street, a reminder of the extent of the original tidal pill. It was here that many ships were built, including the merchant ship 'Carmarthenshire' that was constructed in 1865. It was the first such ship to enter the Japanese harbour of Yokohama. As well as its cargo of Cardiff coal, the ship carried with it the first Western females to be seen by the Japanese population. Soon after the Captain's wife and his daughter set foot on land, images of European fashions appeared on a range of oriental tableware.

In Pembroke Dock Library

People talk inside the big library.
"Where are the interesting books?" said the boy.
People are walking into the library to look at some
books to read.
People are reading some newspapers.
I feel very very very HAPPY
The library is fantastic inside.

Hayden Rendell

2. Yr Adeilad Pwmpio - The Pump House

This quirky red-bricked building stands in the centre of the roundabout leading to Western Way. Although originally built to pump sewage from the town to the Dockyard, it was never actually used for this function. It was found completely unnecessary to have such a pumping system!

In its time, this elegant building has been used as a meeting house, fishing club and a church.

This is also close to the site of the Pier House Hotel, bombed during World War II.

Beautiful Bleak Building

Brown as a walnut and as ancient
As Santa,
Beige and bleak,
Surrounded by grass,
Sat in a flowerbed for a century,
Makes me feel sorry for it,
For it's being destroyed,
The pumphouse in Pembroke Dock.

Pippin Daines McFadden

Prayers in a Pump House

As Sam was learning the Sunday service in the pump
house.
A mix of cream and yellow
A roundabout surrounded in shops and flowers
As old as a church
As bright as a sunset
It was used as a place of God but has been vandalised
I'm proud and annoyed.

Connor O'Neill

Valine

Pier Hotel has been bombed,
I could tell there was something in there.
I could tell by the smell,
It was horrible disgusting
I wished I wasn't there.
Before the bombing started
It was standing there
All welcome to come in
But a few years later I was in there,
Standing in the smoky rubble.

Christy Bowling

This poem is about my great Aunt Valine Bowling who worked as an ambulance driver during the war. She was the first person to enter the Pier Hotel when it was bombed in 1941.

3. Sioe Orllewin Gwyllt Byffalo Bill - Buffalo Bill's Wild West Show

It's difficult to imagine that one of the greatest entertainers of the late 19th Century visited this dockyard town, but Buffalo Bill certainly did!

The spectacular Buffalo Bill Wild West Show was brought to this spot on May 14th 1903. The show, a massive tableau of the Wild West, containing over 500 horsemen, began its performance with a procession from Pembroke Railway Station to this site in Bierspool. This was led by the showman himself, William F. Cody, otherwise known as Buffalo Bill. Among the star attractions was a range of horsemanship featuring Native Americans, sharp shooting exercises and various displays featuring South American gauchos, Bedouin tribesmen and Russian Cossacks.

Buffalo Bill's Dancing Horses

The dancing horses came down the street.
I clapped and clapped.
Clip clop clip clop went the horse's hooves.
What an amazing sight.
I was happy to see the horses dance.

Samantha

4. Mynwent Filwrol Llanion - Llanion Military Cemetery

Few people realise that this is the only Military Cemetery in Wales. It is the last resting place of servicemen and their relatives who were killed or died while serving in the Garrison town. Concealed within the Llanion housing estate, this really is one of Pembroke Dock's 'hidden treasures!

Look out for row of seventeen graves towards the south of the graveyard. These are the graves of soldiers who died in an accidental explosion while practising the techniques of disarming mines. The incident occurred on 28th April 1942. The men killed were nine Royal Engineers, four men from The King's Own Scottish Borderers and four who were serving with The Pioneer Corps.

An incredible footnote – one officer escaped certain death that day when he chose to leave the tragic scene to answer the telephone!

Postcard
Military Cemetery, Pembroke Dock

You and I have stood in other lands where men had fallen, in their thousands. White head stoned, they are 'at ease' in inch perfect rows on shaven lawns. Precise places where the words 'cemetery' and 'symmetry' seemed interchangeable.

But, here, in this overlooked corner of the far west, this final resting place of the brave, feels like a village churchyard. Though the names, those that have not withered, like their young lives, tell of far-off places. On this soft morning their weathered memorials stand ankle deep amongst the daisies and celandines and bluebells. I see, soon to be obscured by the lengthening grass, an inscription 'Thy will be done'. Humph!

George
April 2005

The Yew Tree

I saw each cortege come
Heard marching boots
Muffled drum
The farewell fusillade
Saw comrade set aside his spade
Mourners blink away a tear
And grieve for lives, so short
So sweet, so dearly bought
So vainly lying here
I heard the bugles fade
Brave men resting among my roots
Years unspent, scattered in my shade.

C.G.

5. Y Gwersyll Cytiau -
The Hut Camp

This was once the home to Hut Camp, later known as Llanion Barracks. Originally these barracks, which could house anything up to 1000 men, were built in only six weeks! Infantry regiments from all over the country have occupied these barracks.

The red-bricked barracks we see standing today were built later in 1906. During the Second World War, American GIs of the 110th US Infantry Regiment were based here and this led to a visit from the Supreme Allied Commander, General Dwight D. Eisenhower who arrived here in at Llanion in 1944.

The Barracks have been converted for residential use and the building formerly used by the officers, is now occupied by the Pembrokeshire Coast National Parks Authority and the Countryside Council for Wales.

6. Hobbs Point –
Hobbs Point

Hobbs Point was built by apprentices in 1829 as a 'Fitting Out' area for ships that were built in the Dockyard. They used a diving bell to lay the foundations.

When Telford's road system from St Clears was completed in 1837, Pembroke Dock became a post town and, as such, became an important point for the movement of mail to and from Ireland and Great Britain.

Prior to the building of The Cleddau Bridge, firstly a passenger ferry, then a car ferry operated between Hobbs Point and Neyland.

My Mum's and Nan's Memories

No supermarkets when Nan was young
Mam lived by black dark grey barracks of Llanion.
Now gone new buildings built,
Cleddau Bridge completed,
Ferry Boat took people across water to Neyland.

Danielle Mckelvie.

Wading to Pembroke Dock

Wind whipping Grandad's face
The mast creaking as if to collapse
Climbing down from the battered ship
A passer-by at Cardigan Bay
Offering shelter and warmth
Grandad and others cannot refuse
Sun rising as Grandad sleepily awakens
Next, aboard a motor boat, with flaking paint
Speeding towards Pembroke Dock
A man suggests a short cut
Others do not refuse
The sea sways lazily
Boat stays and does not go
Feet splash in water and wade urgently
Through saphire water tinged with cloudy foam
Until reaching the sandy land of Pembroke Dock

Siân

7. Cae Ffair – Fairground

'Watery Meadows' has seen fun fairs and horse racing events, and the tradition continues to this day.

8. Stryd Flaen–
Front Street

When you walk down Front Street, take a close look at numbers 25 to 28 as these are reputed to be the first houses that were built in Pembroke Dock. Much has changed and it is difficult to believe that this relatively short street once housed seven public houses to serve the hundreds of thirsty dockyard workers! Women from Llangwm would supplement this by steering their boats in this direction in order to sell a range of fish.

A View From Front Street

The houses in Neyland are multi-coloured wobbly boxes.

The Cleddau River is a purple wiggly circular snake. The boats in the water are green jumping fish.

The Cleddau Bridge is a rectangle of a boat upside down with pink and purple spots.

Front Street is special. There are mixes of colours. You can hear all different sounds. And sit and watch the boats go by.

Josephine Cheswick

9. Amgueddfa Tŵr y Gwn – Guntower Museum

This impressive stone structure, built in 1849 – 50 at a cost of £9,230, is situated at the western end of Front Street. This 'Cambridge' Gun Tower is one of only seven in the world, of which seven are to be found in the Haven. Originally built to repel foreign fleets, it is now the town's museum and is definitely worth a visit.

The Gun Tower

I went to the Gun Tower for my Dad's birthday.
It was built in 1849.
It's grey and a bit white.
It was built in Front Street in middle of the water.
As heavy as an elephant.
It makes me feel cold and think about the war.

Stacey Davies

The Gun Tower

Makes me feel safe
Used by soldiers in the war protecting our town,
Grey and black
As big as a cathedral.
It's near the Dockyard in Front Street.
Built in 1849
Makes me feel safe
Because it protects us.

Ryan Llewellyn

The One O'Clock Gun

Looking at a photo I can see a pub
The pub I see is not there now
It's called the Imperial Hotel
A house has took its place
People march to the Barrack Hill to see an amazing
sight
Horse and cart man and child all came to see
The One O'clock gun fired from the Barracks Hill
The Gun Tower was there and is here now
Although it is now a museum.

Benjamin Pearce

Bronze Panels

Round the corner on the Dockyard wall, you can see six relief panels. They were carved in Bath Stone by sculptor Perryn Butler and then cast in bronze, they depict the history of shipbuilding in Pembroke Dock.

The artist grew up in Pembroke Dock, her father was Queen's Harbour Master for Pembroke Dock from 1953 – 1957.

Panel 1 Paterchurch Point (Georgian era)

Panel 2 One day my ship will come (Early Victorian era)

Panel 3 The launch of the 'Osborne' (Mid Victorian era)

Panel 4 Riveting in the big shed (Late Victorian era)

Panel 5 Pay day 1907 (Edwardian era)

Panel 6 Direct Hit 1941 (George the IV)

10. Arwydd Lloches Rhag Bomiau –
Air Raid Shelter Sign

The quaint building at the end of Commercial Row is an excellent example of an early 20th Century shop front. It was the backdrop for a number of scenes of the popular television programme, The Onedin Line.

Next door to the chemists, stood Pembroke Dock's first bank, The Milford Haven Bank. Opposite the shop, sharp eyes will spot a war time air raid shelter sign embedded in a tree.

Moores Chemist Shop

As quiet as a sleeping mouse
Friendly local town.

Mossy creamy shady house
Strange and lonely

Also cheerful
Dreary as darkness

Could be a friendly place
Sometimes damp and dreary

Young woman, long old-dress – lonely face
Scared dark eyes

Looking for medicine for sick son
Can hear his never-ending cries.

Jade Sandford

The First Raid

I lit my candle,
I walked into my room
I climbed into bed
Blew out my candle light
It was turning midnight
Nothing could be heard for miles.
Then a shrieking sound
It was a bomb
I ran to tell my parents
They grabbed me took me to the shelter
I was safe!

Shannon Honeysett

The First Air Raid

Younger child screaming at the siren sound
Rushing to shelter
Somewhere underground

Staring into space – feeling queasy
No expression
Very uneasy

Wish this had never started
Pull back the curtains
So now they're parted

Rushing downstairs to find family
They're rushing upstairs
To find me.

Jade Sandford

11. Capel Y Garsiwn –
Garrison Chapel

Then Garrison or Dockyard Chapel, built in 1831, is considered to be the only Classical Georgian church in Wales.

Built specifically to serve the soldiers based here, one of its most famous worshippers was General Gordon of Khartoum who served with the Royal Engineers. The chapel's most interesting features is its doomed roof and bell tower. The bell, which originally hung here, was cast in Spain, having been captured from a Spanish cruiser!

The chapel later became the Garrison Theatre, then a motor museum before falling into disrepair. To the delight of everyone, the restoration, of the structure, backed by the Heritage Lottery Fund, was completed in 2005.

The Dockyard Chapel

A man sitting on a battered box
The Garrison chapel is battered
As grey as a breeze block
The dome is like half an apple
Today it's a hedgehog
It makes me feel very old.
Hip hip hoorary! Yes the old chapel is being rebuilt.

Billy Wood

12. Awyrennau Môr 'Sunderland' – Sunderland Flying Boats

In 1930, a major part of the dockyard was transferred from the Admiralty to the Air Ministry. The following year, the Royal Air force established a seaplane base, operated by Southampton flying boats of 210 squadron. 1938 saw the arrival of the squadron's first Sunderland flying boats – the aircraft that Pembroke Dock is most associated. During the second World War the Sunderlands fulfilled the important role of protecting British Convoys from the German Navy.

13. Terfynfa'r Fferi – Ferry Terminal

Ireland is only a four-hour journey from the ferry terminal here in Pembroke Dock. The ferry taking you there is the Isle of Innishmore and it is the second largest passenger ferry in Europe.

Irish Ferry

Horizon,
Sea
And Harbour
Engine, sea, wind and people. My mum asking me
questions
I was not answering,
Day dreaming
The sun is sparkling on the water
We're going on holiday.

Irish Ferry

Birds diving for food.
The waves, people talking, the wind and the seabirds.
Good fashion sense
Tall quiet, blue eyes
Sun is shining in the sky.
Clouds just floating by.

I'm on the ferry with my mum and dad,
Going exploring.
Big, white ferry with funnel and lots of windows.

Hollie Thompson

14. Yr Iard Longau Lyngesol Frenhinol – Royal Naval Dockyard

At its peak in the 1890's, the Royal Dockyard was one of the largest in the world, employing over 3,000 people. Over 250 Royal Navy vessels and five royal yachts have been built here over the years. Pembroke Dock can boast many firsts as it built the first steam man-of-war, HMS Tartar and the first propeller-driven warship, HMS Conflict.

Pembroke's Haven

Celts in coracles
Fished creeks and river
Ancient Druids floated bluestones
En route to Stonehenge
Roman traders sailed the tidal reaches
Seeking provisions for its legions.
Viking longships seeking shelter
Settled in the Haven
Becoming part of the nation.

Viking raiders Norman invaders
Felmish traders Kentucky Quakers
Soldiers sailors traders whalers
Differing in language genes and culture
United in marriage and moulded by nature
Into Little Englanders.

Nelson proclaimed the Haven's promise
Great ships and small ships
Made the shipyards famous.
Built on beaches
And in sheltered creeks.
In Pater's Royal Dockyard
For the great British fleets
Royal Yachts and Battleships
Coastal Traders and Cotton Slavers.
Ships of oak driven by sail
Wooden walls clad in steel
And powered by steam.
Built by shipwrights
Skilled craftmen and innovators.
King's ships and merchantmen
Manned by old salts and blue-jackets
In the finest sea-dog tradition.

David Ll. Jones

15. Twr Paterchurch – Paterchurch Tower

Dating back to at least the 13th Century, this is the oldest building in Pembroke Dock. A fine example of a first floor hall tower, there is uncertainty over its original purpose. We know that it was once owned by the knights of St John of Jerusalem. Was it a church, look-out tower or farm? Perhaps it was a combination of all three. Certainly the case for it being a church was strengthened when the walls of the dockyard were extended in 1844. This led to the discovery of an old burial ground next to the tower.

Pembroke Dock was known as Pater until the dockyard became established.

16. Rasys Beiciau Peni-ffardding – Penny Farthing Bike Races

In the 1902 fair, held on this site, Penny Farthing Bicycle Races were held.

17. Llongau Tanfor Y Rhyfel Byd Cyntaf - WWI Submarines

In addition to the many ships that have been built here in the dockyard, the Whitehouse torpedo sheds remind us of the many submarines that were constructed here during the First World War. They included the unlucky L10 which had been built in Pembroke Dock in 1918. Whilst undergoing sea trails off St Ann's Head, the submarine hit the bottom and failed to surface. News of her plight soon reached the dockyard and anxious onlookers waited for her return in the wind and rain. Eventually, after many hours and much to the relief of everyone, it managed to resurface.

Its luck was not to last though, as, a few months later, it was sunk by a German warship!

18. Balwnau Amddiffyn –
Barrage Balloons

This is the site of one of the many Barrage Balloons that were tethered throughout the town during World War Two. One of those in Pennar created some minor havoc when it broke free from its mooring by St Patricks Church and proceeded to float over Bufferland. It knocked off many chimney pots before it could be recovered.

Llanreath Beach

Trees swaying swiftly, slowly
Water dripping off flower peta;s
Beach is sweet, beach is silent
Safe and warm
Llanaeth beach is quiet.

Luci Cole

14. Y Capten Watkin Owen Pell – Captain Watkin Owen Pell

One of the most colourful Dockyard supervisors during the 19th Century was Captain Watkin Owen Pell. He lost his leg in action against the French in 1800 and adopted a wooden replacement. A strict disciplinarian, the Captain would check the work of his men by spying through a telescope from the top of Barrack Hill. His donkey, on which he toured the Dockyard, was trained so well, it would carry him up the gangways onto the decks of the ships under construction.

20. Barics Amddiffynadwy – Defensible Barracks

A schedule II listed building, The Defensible barracks was built to defend the dockyard from a land attack. The building was started in 1841 and completed in 1846. It is claimed that the barracks' overall design was influenced by 16th Century Italian style fortifications. Originally the barracks were known as Treowen Barracks and from here, twice a day, a cannon firing a blank charge would alert town residents lacking watches that it was either noon or nine thirty in the evening. The 9.30 signal became recognised as the curfew for local girls 'out courting.' The noon day and evening guns rang out for the last time in the 1920's.

Serving with the Duke of Lancaster's Own Yeomanry during World War Two, the popular character actor Arthur Lowe (Captain Mainwaring in Dad's Army) found himself stationed here at the Defensible Barracks.

The Barracks

I saw the barracks
When I took my dog for a walk last night
Huge
An incredible moat.
A huge fort towering over you,
The shadow of the building frightening.
Soldiers of the army
Soldiers of the navy.
A ghostly place where no one lives,
Deserted and out of reach.

Danielle Rowe

My Dad Remembers

Defensible Barracks wet and dirty.
Inside lovely and warm
Outside, smells like smoke
Inside, smells like chicken
People get medals
Shining like the suns rays
When turned to chandelier.

Anwen Barrass

21. Tan Tanc Olew –
Oil Tank Fire

The Admiralty built a range of huge oil tanks on this site at Llanreath in 1927. During the War, these tanks were attacked by three German planes, on Monday August 19th 1940. The fire that ensued was one of the greatest infernos of the war. It raged for three weeks and was fought by 650 firemen from brigades all over the country. 11 of the 17 tanks were completely destroyed and five fire fighters from Cardiff lost their lives. A memorial to them is to be found in the middle of the Golf Course.

The Great Tank Fire

All of the pigs fled through the smoke,
You could have just called it smoky bacon.
A very large, white bomber,
Had dropped some small, fierce looking bombs.
The fierce bombs dropped on Barrack Hill,
On the military fuel dumps.
The flames licked quickly at the now, black air.
The smoke lasting three, long weeks.
Everyone was petrified,
Scared,
Frightened.
Firemen risked their lives,
Just to save Pembroke Dock.

Dominic Rogers

Cloud of Smoke

The Bombs dropped on the oil tanks
I felt scared and worried
I could see the flickering flames
Suddenly the biggest explosion Britain has ever seen
happened
The explosion could be heard in Haverfordwest
I could smell smoke and hear the flames
Crackling
Hissing
I saw a big thick cloud of smoke progressing through
Military Road
I ran inside
I felt trapped inside my own home

Thomas KaŸaks

The Last Bomb Dropped

Petrified!
I heard the siren
I was glued to my bed
The silence was broken by the screeching bombs
The cellar is where I hid
Cold and wet
Scared to death.
Boom!
Then the last bomb dropped ...

The First Air Raid

I heard a noise in bed
And my brother said
Don't be scared!
I was more than scared I was petrified!!
My Mum came up
We heard a screech
We looked out of the window
I could feel the heat
It was like a drum
I could see my best friend on the floor
He was …dead!!

Craig Lucas

22. Ffrwydrynnau Tanfor – Submarine Mines

The Government constructed a torpedo store and magazine close to the shore near Pennar Mouth in 1875. Torpedo trails and submarine mining experiments, unique in Wales, were carried out there. The site was also used to store all the equipment necessary to mine the whole of the Haven.

After the Second World War, the site of the torpedo depot became surplus to requirements. The land was sold and converted into Pennar Park Holiday Camp. This has since closed.

23. Cwch Fferi –
Ferry Boat

The Bentlass to Pennar ferry boat service was a major way for farmers' wives to bring their produce to market in Pembroke Dock. Workers who lived on the other side of the Pembroke River also used it.

Tragedy struck on February 8th 1889 when the ferry sank and all nine people on board were drowned. The ferry man, John Jones and his young assistant was returning with seven women on board who had visited the market. The waters had been choppy and the tide was ebbing against a strong wind. The inquest verdict was "that the deceased and those with him met their death by the accidental upsetting of the boat."

Feb 1889

A day like any other
Shawled against the spray
The women with their shopping bags
On this their market day.

Bonnets nodded to their friends
They smile and take their seat
Boarding the familiar boat
As they did every week.

A day like any other
The oars flashed to and fro
From Pennar Bridge to Bentlass
They sat in stoic row.

And chatted their, as old friends do
They could not realise
The two dogs growling in the boat
Would cause it to capsize.

The dogs began their fighting
Around the women's feet
They stood up and with lifted skirts
Began to climb the seats.

"Sit down – sit down!" John Jones did yell
And water filled the boat
And over-board they screamed and fell
Only the shawls did float.

Nine souls were lost that fateful day
In eighteen eighty nine
And many a tear did roll down the cheeks
Of those who were left behind

Many a son and daughter wept
And many a husband died
For those who were drowned on market day
The whole community cried.

Gwen Anderson

24. Jacobs Pill –
Jacobs Pill

This is a corruption of the Welsh Pŵll - meaning pool.

Pirate ships would have been seen passing here on their way up to Pembroke Quay.

Sir Edward Reed established Jacob's Pill Boat Yard in the 1874 as a rival to the Royal Dockyard. After becoming elected MP for Pembroke Borough, he fulfilled his promise of creating a shipyard, offering many jobs to workers recently made redundant. Sir Edward Reed, who had a hand in designing the Royal yacht Osborne, was a prolific boat designer. Perhaps the most famous ship built here was The Hiei, a Corvette built for the Japanese Navy and launched in 1877. By the end of the 19th Century, the yard closed and between the two World Wars an Isolation Hospital was established here.

25. Capel Bethania – Bethany Chapel

With the inception of the Dockyard and the rapid growth of the new town of Pembroke Dock, churches and chapels sprung up to satisfy the growing demands of the town's worshippers. First off the mark were the Baptists who built Bethany Chapel in 1818. They were the first Christian organisation in Pembroke Dock to build a place of worship. Constructed using voluntary labour, the original building had a seating capacity of 350.

In 1877, it was thought that a new building was needed to meet the demands of its growing congregation. A schoolroom was added in 1904-5.

As Tall As A Giant

Different colours of brown
On a corner
As tall as a giant
Cold
The heating's never on
A policeman went there because something was stolen

N Thomas

Pembroke Dock is Colourful

A Colourful boat on the Cleddau
In Bethany Chapel feeling happy
Watching a brother or sister being christened.
Albion School
It's big and old
There's a metal gate to open

Daniel Evans

26. Neuadd y Farchnad – The Market Hall

The Market Hall was built in 1826 and purchased by the Borough Council in 1881. Weekly variety shows were once held in the former courthouse.

Of interest is the old postage stamp machine that can be found on the Eastern wall.

The whole site was recently renovated with the help of a Heritage Lottery grant

27. Ysgol Sgwâr Albion – Albion Square School

Albion Square was the hub of Pembroke Dock. The first Co-op opened here in 1893 and, in nearby Charlton Terrace, was the County Police Headquarters, jail and pound.

In the centre of the square is a memorial lamp, erected in 1914 to commemorate the Royal Dockyard's centenary.

On the South side of the square stands Albion Square Infants School, (now closed), a prime example of a Victorian Board School. Originally the school catered for girls and infants. The boys went to the Old British School in nearby Meyrick Street.

Now and Then

I can see the cane.
I can hear a cane.
I feel scared
I can see flowers
I can hear people talking.
I feel very happy because this school is mine.

Dion Evans

Then and Now

I can see an old school
I can hear old pencils squeaking.
I feel sad.
I can see a pretty classroom.
I can hear my friends talking.
I feel happy in school.

Laura Stokes

28. Bysiau Deulawr - Double Deckers

Silcox had a fleet of red double decker buses, some with cane seats. Ernie James owned and drove a blue single decker bus, the 'Pioneer'. Ernie never left us standing behind at a bus stop no matter how full the bus was. We all loved Ernie – he had a ventriloquists doll and used to take part in local concerts. (See *A Scrap of Local History* Page 68.)

29. Eglwys Gatholig Y Santes Fair – St Mary's RC Church

Reputedly, Catholic dockyard workers, many of whom were Irish immigrants escaping famine, chipped in a day's pay every month in order to build St Mary's in 1847. Some of them provided unpaid labour in its construction. Of interest are the stained glass windows that adorn the eastern wall which were erected in 1926. Buried alongside the church by special dispensation, is the grave of Father Oliver Murphy who served St Mary's as its parish priest for 44 years.

The Building of St. Mary's Church

Feeling cold and miserable
Hungry too.
I can see boats bobbing up and down,
The rain is beating down me.
My Uncle works in the Royal Dockyard
His job is to help build boats.
He paid a pound to help build the church
It took years to build
And is still standing now.

The Building of St. Mary's Church

From Ireland to Pembroke Dock,
Boarding the ship,
Feeling sad, skies miserable,
Funding some jobs for a couple of shillings.
My father and I work in the Royal Dockyard,
I brush the floor, he mends the ships,
We each get paid 10 shillings,
We put 5 shillings each to St. Mary's Church,
The Church took years to build.
It will stand forever.

Thomas Doyle

30. Eglwys Rydd Seion –
Zion Free Church

This beautiful building was once a Wesleyan Chapel. It was built using compensation money received when the Methodists former chapel had to demolished because it stood within a specified distance to the projected Defensible Barracks site.

A growing congregation meant that it had to be enlarged in 1867 to its present imposing structure which seats 1340 people.

The Wesley Chapel, as it became known, was closed and put on the market in 1986. It was purchased and renamed the Zion Free Church.

Prior to this, the chapel's basement was used as the town's library until the building was considered to be unsafe for public use.

31. Sinema'r Grand –
Grand Cinema

The Grand cinema was located at the bottom of Lower Meyrick Street. Part of the St Govan's Centre now occupies the site.

A Scrap of Local History

When I read it in the paper,
My eyes filled up with tears.
They were going to pull 'The Grand' down.
It had been closed for years.
The box office was all boxed in
Where we used to stand and pay,
Vandalised and knocked about,
'The Grand' had had its day.

Many times we caught the bus
And every time we knew
When we hurried into Dimond Street
That we would have to queue.
Right past Taylor's Hardware shop
It stretched if the film was good.
We queued in the sun and queued in the rain,
Hours it seemed we stood.

When at last we reached the door
And shuffled up in line,
"Standing only" came her cry
As she snatched our one and nine.
We propped ourselves against the walls
In straggly, shifting rows,
An usherette with flashing torch
Kept treading on our toes.

Ester Williams dived and swam,
Tarzan swung from tree to tree.
Some films were sad and made you cry,
Most ended happily.
We laughed or wept as film decreed,
Sobbed or shook with mirth.
You may be sure by ten o'clock
We had had our money's worth.

When the National Anthem started,
With the maximum of fuss,
Seats were all tipped smartly back
In the rush for Silcox's bus.
By the time we reached the pavement
The 'decker had long gone
Then Ernie James's Pioneer
Rolled up and crammed us on.

The arrival of our Ernie
Meant relief for aching feet
But by the time we all pushed on
There were four to every seat.
So we stood again on the old blue bus
Like sardines, packed in tight,
Warned that if we saw a policeman
To crouch down out of sight.

A scrap of local history
Has vanished, gone for good.
Just a piece of empty ground
Where once our cinema stood.
When demolition experts
Moved in to clear the land,
I remembered all the grand times
We had in the old 'Grand'.

32. Neuadd Pater –
Pater Hall

The Pater Hall was built on the site of the town's Temperance Hall, which was destroyed by bombing during World War Two. It was said that when the bombs exploded, the main doors of the building flew out and its ornate key was later recovered in Front Street!

The hall is the town's major entertainment and social centre and has a seating capacity of 255. Within the building is the Council chamber, the office of the Town Clerk and a meeting room.

33. Capel Bethel –
Bethel Chapel

When a dissident group from Bethany Chapel's congregation wanted a separate church, they built Bethel Chapel here in 1844. This neo-gothic building, with its 400 seats, had to be re-built in 1872 after a violent gale ripped off part of its roof.

In 1857, it was claimed that Bethel was the first nonconformist church in Pembrokeshire to have a 'keyed instrument' – a harmonium.

34. Canolfan y Coroni – Coronation Centre

It is said that, because of dissension due to the influence of the Church in the Victoria Road National School, the Meyrick Street Old British School was founded. In 1901. This school was demolished and in 1904 it was replaced by the building we see today, the Coronation Boys School. It now serves as the town's Further Education Centre.

Inside the building are two large dramatic murals that depict Pembroke Dock's rich heritage. These were created by Mr George Lewis and were painted with the help of his students.

Coronation Centre

The roof is like a very long slide.
The drainpipe is like a giraffe's neck.
The windows are like a spider.
The coronation centre looks like an office inside and
they do lots of things in there.

Coronation Centre

I'm the grandest of ladies that Meyrick Street's
known
And over a hunderd years old
Though my paint may have peeled and there's damp
in my bones
I'm a treasure (or so I've been told).

I was born here you know, back in 1904
Town's children flocked round just to see
Plus their teachers, the mayor and the Temperance
Band,
Reception especially for me.

For their efforts they each got a round tin of
chocolate
Which bore a portrait of the King
Then medals were given speeches delivered
While children sat round in a ring

You can tell from this tale they thought well of me,
Of tall handsome stature (they said)
Imposing, well, built and of good disposition
An asset, the finest, well bred.

You see they were trusting their children's well-being
To me; think I managed all right
Dear thoughts of those children who came through
my doorway
Are with me by day and by night.

Old ladies have memories and I'm no exception
Recalling that grand 'Golden Age'
When audiences came from all over the county
to see my productions on stage.
They were wonderful times but I'm still going strong
And hope to for many more years
My children grown up now but still I can show them
New practices, starting right here.

Olive Davies

35. Eglwys Blwyf Sant Ioan – St John's Parish Church

St John's parish Church was built in 1847. The 13th Century churches at Tenby and Castlemartin influenced its overall design. This church has fifteen stained glass windows designed by C.E. Kemp and in the Lady Chapel are beautiful examples of carved reredos. One should also note the carved screen that serves as a memorial to the men of the King's Own Light Infantry who had been stationed at Pembroke Dock during the First World War. In addition, at the rear of the church, there is a memorial board listing the names of all those service men from Pembroke Dock who lost their lives in the Second World War.

The peal of bells in the impressive tower was completed in 1902 in commemoration of the coronation of Edward VII.

36. Eglwys Sant Andreas –
St Andrew's Parish Church

Built in an Italian Gothic style in grey squared limestone with prominent red brick and Bath stone features, this building was established in 1866. St Andrews Presbyterian Church has three beautiful stained glass windows, unusual for a Nonconformist church and its large basement that served as a Sunday school could seat 750 children!

The church underwent extensive renovations in 1881, which involved re-roofing and improving the acoustics of the building.

A Wedding

Rough, grey stone
Behind cars, opposite Brian's shop
It's as grey as granite
I am happy
My mum is getting married.

Christopher Butland

Carols in a Church

Grey hard stone
Behind a post box
Hard as stone
I feel like a mouse
The building is big and I am small
The vicar listens to some carols.

Emma Youell

Sid Jenkins the Fish

Fetching the fish
Smelling like rotten old sewage
At Seven Law Street
I was selling the fish
And have a little bit of a chat
The fish all cold and wet`
You could taste the fish
Another day over and back home to give news.

Liam Marshall

This Poem is about my great Grandad Sid Jenkins, the fish who lived at 3 Law Street

37. Y Parc Coffa –
Memorial Park

The Memorial Park opened in 1925 and commemorates the "fallen heroes of Pembroke Dock who gave their lives in the 1914-18 Great War."

The gates and clock were erected in memory of two young men who were killed in the air raids of 1941. One was aged 18, the other a mere 14.

During the Second World War, a large part of the park was ploughed up as part of the Dig For Victory campaign. The idea was to grow onions, but nothing grew. Eventually the ground was deemed unsuitable for growing any kind of vegetable!

38. W. Haggar – Arloeswr y Sinema – W. Haggar – Pioneer of Cinema

Arthur William Haggar (1851-1925) was a true pioneer of cinema. He was also a showman and fairground proprietor. He and his large family travelled throughout Britain bringing entertainment to the people. Here at Station Field his Electric Bioscope, waxworks and theatrical shows regularly took place to entertain the people of Pembroke Dock. His grandson, Len Haggar later ran cinemas in Pembroke, Milford Haven, Cardigan and Pembroke Dock.

39. Gorsaf Reilffordd –
Railway Station

Pembroke Dock station opened in 1864, offering a free ride to Tenby on its inaugural journey. The railway line cut through the town into the dockyard. A secondary spur leading to Hobbs Point followed in the 1870's. Haggar's 1908 film The Life and Death of Charles Peace used the station as its main location. Not only was the film the first 'chase' movie ever made, predating the more famous Keystone Cops films by a number of years, it was also the first film to show a death scene. Based on a true story, the film was a huge sensation and made the Haggar family very wealthy.

The station is still operating and its former office and waiting room have been transformed into a public house.

It Fell Right Beside Me

It fell right beside me,
Someone shouted "It's a hot air balloon!"
It was big, white and it smelled of gas.
There were tons of people,
All watching the massive balloon.
There was silence.

Emily Kaijaks

A Hundred Years Ago

A balloon landed in Pembroke Dock
A hundred years ago,
It fell out of the sky like an eagle hunting for prey
Everyone came out of houses
To see what had happened.
All you could smell was gas
From the abandoned balloon
I didn't know what to say!

Ben Steele

A Small Piece of Heaven

His free-flowing blood
Beneath a rib of our Lord,
This Garden of Eden
A small piece of Heaven
What more do we need?
Where is this place?
Pembroke Dock.

Pauline Phillips

Pembroke Dock 2005

I write as a pure stranger
Who does not share your history
A newcomer, not even Welsh.
First impressions of the Dock
Were stark and grey,
Under a leaden sky.
Snow thawing on the pavements,
Oh for a few front gardens to soften
Or pots of pastel paint,
Or trees along the roads.
Then I discover stone buildings
Chapels, churches, schools
Of great clean beauty
Solid as standing stones in their simplicity.
What amazes me is the welcome and the warmth
Hardly felt elsewhere,
Of those who live behind these walls
I wait to learn the highs and lows
Of your past, of history's overtones,
So complex I can hardly understand.
You've seen glorious days,
Of launching ships at the seas edge
And terrifying ones of battles and
Bombs and fires.
This is not the end of the journey.
Who knows what will come?
The time of the 'Valorous' and 'Ariadne'
That started years of great prosperity
May yet happen anew in the days ahead.

Rhoda Hodes

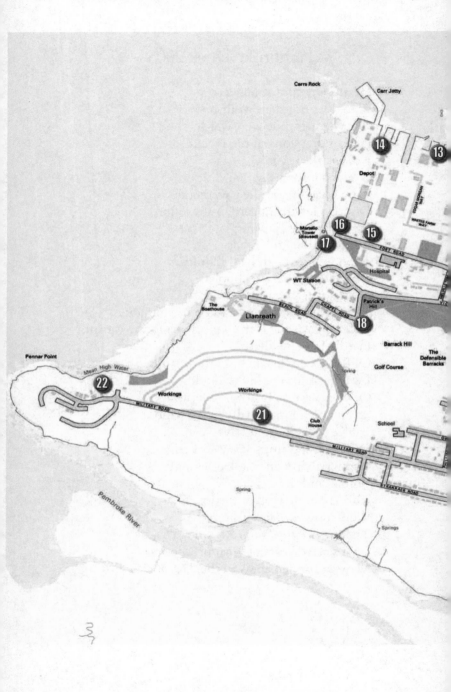

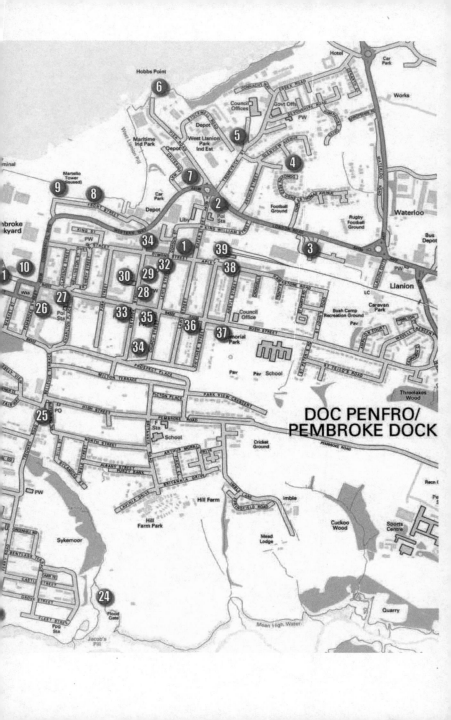

DOC PENFRO/
PEMBROKE DOCK

Guide to Pembroke Dock Town Trail